T0146930

HE WENT A LITTLE FARTHER

STORIES OF CHALLENGE AND
INSPIRATION FROM THE STREETS OF
AN AMERICAN INNER-CITY

STEVE CAMPBELL

WESTBOW
PRESS®
A DIVISION OF THOMAS NELSON
& ZONDERVAN

WestBow Press books may be ordered through booksellers or by contacting:

WestBow Press
A Division of Thomas Nelson & Zondervan
1663 Liberty Drive
Bloomington, IN 47403
www.westbowpress.com
844-714-3454

ISBN: 979-8-3850-0845-2 (sc)
ISBN: 979-8-3850-0846-9 (hc)
ISBN: 979-8-3850-0847-6 (e)

Library of Congress Control Number: 2023918177

Print information available on the last page.

WestBow Press rev. date: 10/23/2023

To all those who, on a daily basis, are willing to "go on a little farther" in order to serve those who cannot help themselves. Thank you.

A special dedication goes to all of the ministry volunteers and partners who gave of themselves to help us "go on a little farther." Thank you from the depths of my heart.

FOREWORD

I admit that I am a cynic when it comes to Christian leaders. I earned the right. For twenty years, I worked in professional evangelical ministry. I was a reporter for a nationally broadcast Christian television show, which put me on the front lines of Christian celebrity. By the way, this is not that different from secular celebrity. I saw the very humanness of the most familiar faces of America's holy, and many times they weren't, well, holy. In fact, I began to gain great hope that if God could use these flawed vessels, then maybe, just maybe, he could use me.

It was on one of those production assignments that I met Steve and Wanda Campbell. It was 1989 and they were in the early years of loving the homeless and discarded of urban Columbus, Ohio. That was thirty-two years ago. Over the past three decades, I have watched their ministry grow in reach and focus. I have heard the stories of lives touched and changed. I have seen and met these people. I have stood side by side with the Campbells, serving food to the homeless on Thanksgiving Day. I have watched them speak tenderly to and wrap their arms around men and women who didn't smell good, didn't dress well, and carried their homes on their backs. I have watched them step aside from the "baby" they birthed and trust it to the hands of a new generation of leadership because they trust the God who breathed the original vision into reality.

I want to tell you the side you don't see. After leaving television, I obtained my real estate license. Steve and Wanda were one of my earliest clients. Because I'm a Christian and advertise on Christian radio, I am called on to provide real estate services to many local Christian leaders and pastors. This made me develop a mantra that I still believe: "If you want to know who someone really is, observe the person when money is involved and no one is watching." Being a realtor often gives me a front-row seat of the inner workings of people's lives, closets, and pocketbooks.

In the sale and purchase of several homes, I saw the Campbells do the right thing—every time. When corners could be cut, when promises could be half-kept, when leverage could be used to back off of contractual obligation, when no one would know but me, the Campbells insisted on doing the right thing— every time. Lest one think that is normal, it is not. Virtually every other homeowner would certainly do what is *legal,* but Steve and Wanda understand that what is *right* is often beyond what is legal, and they insist on it. That speaks volumes to me.

I have told my husband that if I happen to die before either of the Campbells, I want them to speak at my funeral. Why? Because the man and woman you will learn about in this book defy my cynicism, restore my hope in the ability of humans to serve God without ego, and demonstrate a Christianity that I hope can be said of me.

Read, laugh, learn, and be inspired because these stories are the threads of fabric that, when woven together, reveal the humble and sacrificial lives of two incredible people about whom I am *not* cynical. It is a privilege to know them.

Kathy Chiero Greenzalis
CEO and Founder, DownSize Columbus
Keller Williams Greater Columbus Realty
Former News Anchor and Reporter, Pat Robertson and *The 700 Club*

ENDORSEMENTS

Steve Campbell is one of the most gifted storytellers I know. For untold hours, I've listened to and learned from Steve's incredible wealth of wisdom gained from decades of faithful and humble service. He is one of my most trusted friends and encouraging mentors, and I hope to be even half the man that Steve has been and continues to be. You will be challenged, inspired, and encouraged as you read through each of these real-life stories. They are drenched with the pain, suffering, and hardship of life, as well as the overwhelming grace and mercy of Jesus, and told by a man who has walked in unimaginable strength, unwavering conviction, and uncommon humility.

Chad Fisher
Founding and Lead Pastor, Rock City Church

Pastor Steve is a master storyteller. From my very first encounter with him, I wanted to learn to tell stories like he does. Over the last thirty years, I discovered it was not the stories I wanted to imitate but the man himself. This powerful book reveals the stories of Jesus as he graciously invited Steve and Wanda into his work. Jesus miraculously gave them "eyes to see the need and hearts to meet the need." As you read these amazing stories, maybe you can begin by praying that the Lord will give you the same eyes and heart. My desire to be more like Steve continues because, in doing so, I will be closer to Jesus. As he records in these pages, may we one day also say, "I dreaded my encounters with him, served him anyway, endured his unpleasantries and…soon led him to Jesus."

Todd R. Marrah, PhD
Superintendent, Tree of Life Christian Schools
Direction Team Pastor, Rock City Church
Board Member, Columbus Dream Center
Chairman of the Board, Association of Christian Schools International

I believe Jesus was the greatest storyteller who ever lived, but Steve Campbell is one of the best in this generation. Steve has that rare ability to draw you into the story, from being an observer to being on the inside. When you combine Steve's gift of storytelling with his decades of street ministry, you have the ingredients of this book. It shows us what happens when the gospel of Jesus confronts the pain of life in the inner city today. I have no doubt that this book will strengthen your faith, restore your hope, and increase your love, especially for those who might seem very unlovable!

Duane Fleming
Founding Pastor, Christian Community Church of Columbus
Director, Christian Connect Network

Pastor Steve is a master storyteller. He and his wife Wanda spent more than thirty years ministering throughout the streets in the heart of Columbus, Ohio. Because of their hearts for the hurting and underserved, their desire to see God move, and their willingness to do God's work, many people have experienced true life transformation in those thirty years. The stories in this book are inspiring. They will benefit any believer who desires to be the hands and feet of Jesus to the lost and hurting.

Cris Gordon
Executive Director, Columbus Dream Center

A must read for every follower of Jesus! This is real life Jesus stuff! You will be challenged to go beyond your own comfort zone. These stories of God's love and power will push you to trust God beyond your own convenience and abilities and experience real living for your Savior.

Scott Jackson
President, Thrive Christian Leadership Foundation

ACKNOWLEDGMENTS

My wife and soulmate Wanda

Throughout not only this project but all of our years of ministry, Wanda has been my helper, proofreader, a much-needed critic, and my greatest encourager. Without her support, this project would not have happened.

Alison Hooper

I doubt a writing project is ever any better than the person who edits it. Alison's guidance and expertise have proven invaluable. I asked her to "give my writing a good bath, without scrubbing my voice out of it." She not only "nailed it," but she has been a true joy to work with and has become a most-valued friend to both Wanda and me.

Larry Reed, Sanctuary Video Productions

Larry is both a close colleague and a trusted Christian brother. He created the videos that accompany each story in the book and shot most of the photographs included as well. Sanctuary Video Services is located in Bellevue, Ohio. As a matter of

Christian service, Larry is heavily involved in reentry work for those who have been incarcerated.

Ronald McCauley, U.M.C. Pastor, retired

For fifty years Ron served as a United Methodist Church pastor as well as a District Superintendent. Post-retirement, he served for twelve years as Chaplain for St. Joseph's Hospital in Buckhannon, West Virginia. He authored the book *Morning Prayers* and co-authored the book *Sacred Spaces*.

I am most grateful to Ron for sharing his gift of writing by authoring the prayers in this book. At present, Ron and his wife Peg reside in Lakeside, Ohio.

The Encouragers

To the countless numbers of people who have said, "You should write a book," your words have not fallen on deaf ears. Thank you for your encouragement, your support, and your friendship.

The Givers

To those who gave exceptional financial gifts toward the end that this book might be published, thank you for your generosity. May the Lord bless you as your gifts have blessed others.

Listen! Obedience is better than sacrifice, and submission is better than the fat of rams.

—1 SAMUEL 15:22 (NLT)

INTRODUCTION

I thought it was an innocent question.

After thirty-two years of street ministry in the notorious Short North District of Columbus, Ohio, Wanda and I were on a two-week break on Anna Maria Island. It was late in the day, and I was sitting alone on a bench, looking at a gorgeous Gulf Coast sunset. My heart was postured in prayer when under my breath I asked, "Lord, is there anything you want me to do for you?"

The question was loaded with possibility, though at the time, I hardly expected a response.

After an uncomfortable pause, I felt the Lord's Spirit say to mine, "Well, what haven't you done that I already told you to do?"

I knew exactly what God meant. A zinger to my heart, the message was clear. He was saying, "Why should I ask you to do anything else when you have not yet done what I already told you to do?"

And there was no doubt about what God meant by what "I already told you to do."

I knew exactly what he was talking about.

Bowing my head with the sun setting before me, I stayed postured in prayer. "Okay Lord, I'll do it. I'll write the book. You've asked me to write about the work I have seen you do in the lives of the people of the streets, and I'm sorry that it has taken me until now to obey."

Obedience really is better than sacrifice.

> *He went on a little farther* and bowed his face to the ground, praying, "My Father, if it is possible, let this cup of suffering be taken away from me. Yet, I want your will to be done, not mine."
> —Matthew 26:39 (NLT); emphasis added

Finally, here it is: a book of twelve stories of challenge and inspiration from the streets of an American inner-city.

You will find yourself inspired by stories like "Irv" and challenged by "The Girl at the Dumpster." These stories will reveal how Jesus, who "went a on a little farther" for us, leads us to "go on a little farther" for him.

The common link of these twelve stories is that they all took place between Thanksgiving Day and Christmas. They did not all occur in the same year, but they did occur within the holiday season. They are written in a devotional format, and while each takes place during the holidays, the stories promise to meet you right where you are anytime of the year.

As an added bonus, each story contains a link that will take you to a video presentation of the story. If you are reading this in print, you can view all of our video stories via The Journey of Life Facebook page or at www.thejourneyoflife.org.

And with this obedient offering, I pray that you enjoy the journey, and I hope you will be challenged, inspired, and led to "go on a little farther."

Steve Campbell

Scan the QR Code for a bonus video.

> He went on a little farther and bowed his face to
> the ground, praying, "My Father, if it is possible,
> let this cup of suffering be taken away from me.
> Yet, I want your will to be done, not mine."
>
> —MATTHEW 26:39 (NLT)

IRV

When I first saw him sitting on the gray stone wall, it crossed my mind that he might be the eighth wonder of the world. After all, how could anyone be that drunk and not fall off that wall?

Each night, he sat on that wall and drank until he passed out. The sole survivor of an apartment fire, he was not easy to look at. I later learned that he survived by climbing into a bathtub on the third story of the burning building, sucking the air out of the tub's drain until he was rescued. One ear and most of his lips were missing. His shirt was almost always stained with vomit, slobber, and everything he had eaten in the last three weeks. Every night he sat on that wall, swaying back and forth in a half-conscious stupor, mumbling memories of his past.

His name was Irv.

Most nights, I prayed a brief prayer over him and stuck one of our ministry business cards in his pocket. I hoped he would come visit our small storefront on High Street.

Then it happened. One afternoon, Irv wandered in while mumbling to himself. He got a cup of coffee, walked over, and sat down in my only good chair (a gold velvet Flexsteel rocker). Then he passed out, spilled his coffee, and wet his pants—all on my prized chair.

The Lord reminded me that he had just answered my prayers.

It wasn't long before I realized that Irv was a lot easier to love when he was passed out. When conscious, Irv was really disagreeable. The food we served never seemed to suit him. The things we gave him were never what he wanted. Once he cussed me out because I gave him a brand-new pair of pants. They were blue, and he wanted green. This came from a man whose only shoes in thirty years came from a garbage dumpster—a fact soon to be important.

I have to confess: I grew to hate Irv's guts. For two and a half years, seven days a week, I found Irv on the street. I knew that every night when I went to the Short North District, that old man was going to be there, and nothing I could do would ever satisfy him. I dreaded my encounters with him, served him anyway, endured his unpleasantries, and grew to hate him for it—as if he was the one whose idea this had been in the first place.

The Short North District streets were riddled with folks who were hard to love.

Meanwhile, we had come to know a nineteen-year-old hooker, someone we shared Jesus with and who was entangled in the trafficking lifestyle. Though she wanted the freedom offered to her by a faith in Jesus, the prostitution had a strong hold on her. She climbed into a truck with a guy to turn a trick, and he slit her throat, stuffed her in a garbage bag, and dumped her body in a creek bed on the west side of town. Her mother didn't want her body, but an aunt took custody of her niece's body. We also happened to know the aunt, and she asked us to do the funeral service for her niece. It was a powerful service with nineteen of the girl's friends and family accepting Christ.

In the midst of the service, Irv wandered in. During the invitation to receive Christ as Savior, Irv raised his hand and accepted God's eternal gift.

I'm not saying that Irv became easy to like after that, but it wasn't long before he took it upon himself to greet the newcomers. When a new person came through the front door of our little center, Irv got right up in the person's face, and through his impeded speech and with breath that had never known mouthwash, proclaimed, "Since I come here, I don't dwink no more!"

It wasn't the worst testimony I'd ever heard.

In our yearly Christmas newsletter, we included a list of items that people needed, and our ministry partners and Dream

Builders responded by supplying those items. More than anything else, Irv wanted one thing: a pair of "bwack dress shoes, size 10W." Irv pestered me and pestered me about those shoes. Even though we did not have a clothing ministry and in those days we did not supply shoes, Irv was adamant about his request. So I put shoes for Irv on the Christmas list.

December 23 arrived and so had all the Christmas gifts—all except for one item. Yep, you guessed it: a pair of "bwack dress shoes, size 10W."

I asked God why the shoes hadn't come in, and I heard his answer speak to my heart.

"Steve, I want you to buy those shoes."

So there I was at 3:30 in the morning the day before Christmas, shopping at an all-night discount store for a pair of shoes. I scoured the entire department only to find one pair of "bwack dress shoes, size 10W" at the bottom of a stack of shoes. And the kicker? They were the most expensive shoes in the entire store! God has such a sense of humor.

Christmas Eve afternoon, I took the shoes to Irv. If you remember, I told you that in thirty years, he never had a pair of shoes that did not come out of a garbage dumpster. I soon discovered that "10W" was just a number to Irv. He had no idea what size shoes he wore. However, Irv was determined; he was going to put his size 11 feet into those size 10 shoes.

When Irv got his feet into those shoes, unlaced and tongues standing straight up, a crooked grin spread across his face. Like Frosty the Snowman when he put the silk hat on his head, Irv began to dance in circles. He turned to me slowly and said words I'd never before heard him say: "T'ank you! T'ank you! T'ank you!"

Three months later, Irv pulled me up under one sweat-stained arm and Wanda under the other. He pressed us against his stained shirt that had not been washed in months and said, "Steve, I really, really love you guys!"

Those were the last words I heard Irv say. The police found him dead three days later.

I preached Irv's funeral. As I reflect, I am so glad that Irv came to know Jesus as his Lord. I'm glad that he found a family in our ministry. And I believe Irv is dancing with Jesus today in a white robe and a pair of "bwack dress shoes, size 10W."

But the person who truly benefited the most was me. I received much more from Irv than he received from me. The Lord used Irv to stretch me far beyond my comfort zone and to break my hardened heart into something he could remold for his purpose.

God used Irv to teach me to be willing to "go just a little farther." I am convinced that the voice of God calling each of us to "go just a little farther" is one of the greatest calls put on our lives. I am thankful to God that he gives us Irvs to serve so that we can be molded for his purpose and "go just a little farther," both in the lives of others and in our very own hearts.

Read Matthew 1:18–24.

In our theme verse (Matthew 26:39), Jesus was required to "go on a little farther" than he wanted in order to bring us salvation. He was forced to trust God and leave his comfort zone.

1. When Joseph found out that Mary was pregnant, how was he forced to trust God and "go on a little farther" beyond his comfort zone?
2. In what way might God be asking you to "go on a little farther" out of your comfort zone?

Prayer

O loving God, you have given me life, and you continue to pour over me the power to become a new person each day.

The coolness of your Spirit's wind gives me breath, and the grace of your Spirit enkindles in me a love for you and others.

Come to me this day, and make me ready for your surprises in the midst of the broken pieces of my life.

Help me to stretch beyond my comfort zone by following your loving nudge, and help me to fully surrender myself to you, your words, and your desires for me.

It is then that I sit in your embrace, like a content child on a mother's lap.

Thanks be to God. Amen.

Scan the QR code for a bonus video.

> **"For I was hungry, and you fed me, I was thirsty, and you gave me a drink. I was a stranger, and you invited me into your home…I tell you the truth, when you did it to one of the least of these my brothers and sisters, you were doing it to me."**
>
> —MATTHEW 25:35, 40 (NLT)

THE STREET SWEEPER

Have you ever felt really good about something you've done?

Maybe you thought, *This turned out sooo good!* or *How could it ever get any better than this?* And then, life hands you an epiphany—an "aha moment."

Our first Thanksgiving Day in the Short North District proved to be one of those moments.

The first annual Great Short North Thanksgiving Feast had been so successful. It was over the top! We served home-cooked turkey, dressing, ham, and all the trimmings to sixty-five people. The little center on High Street had come so far, having been open just seven months.

It had been a long and full day, and I was feeling pretty good. I thought, *How could it ever get any better than this?*

Our storefront at 1129 North High Street didn't have a furnace, let alone a kitchen. In order to make room for the tables and chairs needed for the dinner, we found storage for what little furniture we owned. Working from the back end of a box truck parked on a crime-ridden street, we kept the food warm by using hot plates. I chained two gasoline generators to the rear axle of the truck to provide power for the hot plates. The chains kept people from stealing both the generators and the truck.

Now the dinner was over. The mess was cleaned up and the food was stored. The furniture was back in place. After a thirteen-hour day, I was more than ready to go home.

I glanced at my watch. It was 6:30 at night, and snow had been falling for an hour. The sidewalks were covered, and the roads were slick, which meant my trip home would be a slow one.

That's when I heard a knock on the front door—a knock that changed my life.

Shivering and standing in the cold was a little man wearing fatigue pants, a T-shirt, and an army cap. By his side was a wagon containing a push broom and a scoop shovel—the business he pulled along with him wherever he walked.

He swept parking lots and sidewalks for two to three dollars per job, earning just enough to keep himself going. I knew him only as the Street Sweeper.

I opened the door and invited him to come in, out of the snow and the cold.

"Nah!" he said. "Dey told me down da street that you was serving dinner. But I can see you're already closed."

"Hey, come on in!" I insisted. "I still have plenty of food. It's no problem."

"Nah, I know ya want to go home. Go on. I be okay."

It became obvious that I wasn't going to persuade him to come in and eat. He finally agreed to allow me to fix him a meal he could take with him. I piled two plates full of ham, turkey, dressing, and potatoes, both mashed and sweet. I took a whole pumpkin pie and put whipped cream over all of it. I even made him a thermos full of fresh coffee.

He thanked me and ventured off into the now very dark night. The snow was about three inches deep.

As I closed the door behind him, I felt really good about how I had gone the extra mile for the Street Sweeper.

I climbed into the big truck to head home. Once again, I congratulated myself. *How could it ever get any better than this?*

I turned onto Fourth Avenue and peered through the Currier and Ives snowflakes that were falling around the abandoned supermarket on the corner.

In the parking lot, adjacent to the empty building, was a dumpster with a single light hanging over it. Beneath the light and by the dumpster, I saw the Street Sweeper.

Half-covered by snow, he was sitting in his wagon, head bowed and holding his dinner in his lap. He was thanking God for what he had. My heart broke!

At that moment, I experienced an epiphany, an "aha moment" that has stayed with me all these years.

My focus had been on what a good thing I was doing by going out of my way in order to feed this homeless man. After all, hadn't I inconvenienced myself?

But what was it Jesus had said? "The one who wants to be a leader among you must be a servant" (Matthew 20:26). In that moment, I realized that if I was going to truly follow Christ, I was going to have to "go on a little farther." I needed to adopt the heart of a servant. I needed to adopt an attitude that asked, "What can I do to be helpful?" and a lifestyle that modeled, "How might I serve you?"

Many years have passed since that evening, but the Street Sweeper still lives in my heart. Hundreds of thousands of people have been served by the once little center we started in the Short North District. However, few have spoken as strongly into my life's journey than this quiet little man of few words.

Every time I think about the Street Sweeper, I am reminded of the privilege we share when we serve others. I have learned that serving others is far more than just a responsibility I must bear as a Christian.

Serving others is a gift, an opportunity that Christ has extended to us (Matthew 25:35–40). What a privilege it is to actually model Christ!

Will not our lives be more fulfilling? Won't we experience the true meaning of such holidays as Thanksgiving and Christmas on a regular basis if we make serving others a priority value of daily life?

Read Luke 2:6–7.

Even though the Bethlehem innkeeper is often depicted in Christmas plays, he is actually not mentioned in the scripture accounts of Jesus's birth. Luke 2:6–7 tells us that "She [Mary] wrapped him snugly in strips of cloth and laid him in a manger, because there was no lodging available for them."

1. When you think of the Bethlehem innkeeper, whoever he may have been, do you think of him as someone who did all he could to accommodate the birth of Jesus, or do you think of him as someone who should have done more?

2. Is there an area of your life in which you feel God is calling you to serve him more deeply? If so, what step(s) do you need to take in order to fulfill the service to which God is calling you?

Prayer

Gentle and loving God, I give you thanks for always hearing me with love and understanding. I give you thanks for feeling my pain and for taking my cares into your great heart. Wipe clean my tarnished soul, give me a fresh hope, and put a new song on my lips.

Help me not to be afraid of the darkness that hovers over this world.

Grant me some of your courage to move through each day within this crazy world—a world full of hope that is shattered again and again with disappointments.

Place me in the garden of your presence and then make me fit to kneel before you.

Allow me the grace to see you more clearly each day and follow you wherever you lead.

Thanks be to God, Amen.

Scan the QR Code for a bonus video.

> **For the Son of Man came to seek and save those who are lost.**
>
> —LUKE 19:10 (NLT)

DA'NEEN

Rarely have I felt as out of place as I did on my first night of ministry on High Street. The then notorious Short North District of Columbus, Ohio was not in my comfort zone. North High Street was a maze of hookers, johns, dealers, and hustlers, with a few gangs thrown in for good measure.

At heart, I was still a country boy from Kansas. The inner city scene made me very uneasy. The sidewalk in front of the building I had recently rented still bore the bloodstains of the man murdered there just days before—a grim reminder of the reality of life and death in the Short North District of the 1980s.

Unlike the trendy arts and fashion district that it is today, the 1980s version of the Short North on High consisted of a mile-long string of vacant buildings, slum apartments, bars where trouble could easily be found, and a few restaurants where even the rodents were afraid to eat.

Easing past the hookers working in front of the Caravan, a bar that police referred to as "the toilet," I headed south toward the heart of the city. A couple of blocks down the street, I passed Alice Faye's, a biker bar and the kind of a place where if you didn't have a gun, they would give you one.

It was there that I saw her for the first time.

She would have been tall even without the four-inch red heels. A matching red, mid-thigh skirt and the white, too-tight sweater left no doubt as to why she was out here doing the stroll. She wasn't Julia Roberts, but she would attract her share of johns before the night was over.

As I passed her, it struck me: she was no she!

She was David Lee Drake, the most notorious prostitute on High Street.

A transvestite who stood well over six feet in heels, his street name was Da'Neen.

I had no idea how our lives would intertwine over the next few years or how often David would present me the opportunity to "go on a little farther." But I did know David was part of the reason God had called me to the Short North.

I had read about David, a.k.a. Da'Neen, in a series of newspaper articles. Even though he had full-blown AIDS, he was selling his body to any man wanting to have sex with him. Any night of the week, he could be found strolling High Street, picking up tricks.

He bragged to the newspaper reporter, "Ain't nobody can stop me! It ain't against the law to have AIDS!"

When I heard that, I thought, *Somebody will slit his throat and stick him in a dumpster!*

Then God's Spirit spoke into my heart: "You know the only thing wrong with him is that he doesn't know me."

Years later, I realize that God used the voice of David Lee Drake to beckon me to the Short North.

Snapping back to reality, there he was right in front of me. I didn't have the courage to just walk right up to him and start a conversation. However, I did begin to pray—pray for David and for my personal boldness.

Three months passed before I developed the courage to walk up and begin talking to David.

He knew who I was. I was the "preacher man" who led his personal bodyguard to "religion."

David liked to talk trash and act out in front of me. He wanted to impress and intimidate me. Yet when he was arrested and jailed, I was the one he called.

It was late at night when I finally saw David in the jail. It was also the first time I saw David for who he really was.

Wearing an orange jumpsuit instead of a sweater and skirt, David sat in front of me. No make-up, no wig, no heels—just a frail man, street-worn and ill.

I didn't preach at David that night. I simply tried to be his friend.

After he got out of jail, David would occasionally visit our little center on High Street. Always dressed in full drag as Da'Neen, he never stayed long. Most often he was there only long enough to eat a meal.

One winter night, just before Christmas, David, dressed as Da'Neen, walked nonchalantly into our center. He was looking for some aspirin. He had gone to the Dollar Store down the street, and when his attempts to shoplift the aspirin were thwarted, he came to our place and asked Wanda if she had any.

During the course of getting the aspirin, Wanda inquired, "David, wouldn't you like me to pray for you? God can heal that headache."

"Yes ma'am." Sitting down, David opened up to Wanda like he had probably never opened up to anyone before.

Sitting there in that little store front, David asked Jesus to come into his life and to forgive him for all he had done.

David Lee Drake's personal journey of life was anything but smooth. It was neither easy nor glamorous. David made a lot of bad decisions. Those bad decisions led to his death not long after his Christmas encounter with Jesus.

Bad decisions can have life-long or even life-ending consequences. However, those bad decisions do not have to define our eternity.

It is not who we are or how we earn a living that matters when we meet Jesus. It doesn't matter if you are living in the tent house or the penthouse, in a high-rise or the very gutters of life.

It doesn't matter what you've done. Really, it doesn't. What does matter is what you do when you encounter Jesus.

On the night Jesus was born, some shepherds encountered him. They told others and before too long, there were wise men worshiping the Christ Child.

Jesus came to earth to encounter people, and to change our lives by forgiving our sins and giving us eternal life with him in heaven.

David Lee Drake died in a nursing home. He died of AIDS—AIDS that he contracted working as a male prostitute called Da'Neen.

But David Lee Drake didn't die as Da'Neen. Da'Neen died the night David and Wanda prayed together.

God stretched his arms across the expanse of heaven and into the heart of a high-crime district to reach a male prostitute named David Lee Drake. As a result of his encounter with Jesus, David Lee Drake did not die and cease to exist. Today, David Lee Drake lives with Jesus.

Read Luke 2:15–17 and John 3:16.

1. After their encounter with Jesus, the Bethlehem shepherds told everyone what happened to them. How would you describe your personal encounter with Jesus?
2. The underlying issue in David Lee Drake's life was not that he was bad; it was that he was lost. In what way does that relate to your own life?

Prayer

How mysteriously you work, O God. You show me that even the smallest seed has eternal potential so long as it is planted with true faith.

I promise this day to pay attention to the tiniest seed of hope.

I know I need your forgiveness.

My faith, though sometimes small, tells me that Jesus is your son, he died for my sins, and you raised him to life.

I am ready to trust him as my Savior and follow him as my Lord.

O God, guide my life and help me to do your will.

Take my tiny seed of faith, in Jesus's name, and allow me to live with you forever.

Loving God, you are without change. Help me to stretch and grow but always and ever remain yours. When I am with you, I stand on holy ground.

Thanks be to God, Amen.

Scan the QR Code for a bonus video.

> Anyone who belongs to Christ has
> become a new person. The old life
> is gone; a new life has begun.
>
> —2 CORINTHIANS 5:17 (NLT)

A HOOKER FOR CHRISTMAS

A phone call at 11:30 p.m. on Christmas Eve is never a good thing. It is usually a sign that someone needs help.

"Steve, this is Lisa. I'm in trouble! You gotta come get me!"

My first thought was, *Come on Lisa! It's 11:30 on Christmas Eve! The ministry is closed for Christmas. I'm finally home enjoying my family. Why should your bad planning be my emergency?*

The thought of Lisa being in trouble did not come as a surprise. Lisa was pretty in a streetwise sort of way. She was a friend of former gang leaders we had led to Christ. Their encouragement had led the sixteen-year-old prostitute to our High Street storefront. She came to us directly from jail.

Still a teenager, she already had a long string of run-ins with the law, and she was no stranger to the court system. Masked behind her impish smile was a back-alley tough addict and a street-smart hooker.

Lisa was suspicious of everyone and everything. She didn't give her trust to anyone, and she would do anything for a price.

Our first attempts to befriend Lisa were met with cautious resistance. The notion that we cared about her, let alone that God cared about her, was beyond her comprehension.

She needed help, but she didn't want to let anyone get close enough to hurt her. Like any victim of sexual abuse, she had already experienced enough hurt to last a lifetime.

In time, my wife Wanda and the other ladies who worked with us managed to gently break through the wall Lisa had built around her life.

One night, she prayed, asking Jesus to forgive her wrongdoings and to help her straighten out the mess that was her life. As Lisa left that night, Wanda encouraged her. "Lisa, anytime you are in trouble, call on the name of Jesus and he will help you."

Neither had any idea how important that advice would prove to be.

Unknown to us, Lisa had stiffed a drug dealer for two-thousand dollars' worth of cocaine. Not exactly a great career move for anyone.

On Christmas Eve, the irate dealer caught up with Lisa on the streets of the Short North District. He abducted her at gunpoint, forced her into his car, and headed down the interstate to a place where he planned to shoot her and dump her body.

With the car racing down the highway, Lisa suddenly remembered Wanda's counsel: "Lisa, anytime you are in trouble, call on the name of Jesus and he will help you."

Without a second thought she screamed, "Jesus! Help me!," forced the door open, and jumped out of the speeding car.

She landed on the berm, tumbled head over heels, and rolled to the bottom of the embankment. Her clothing was torn, but Lisa suffered only a few bumps and bruises that would serve as a reminder not to do that again.

Sticking to back streets and alleyways, she managed to work her way back to a crack house on Buttles Avenue, from which she called me on Christmas Eve and said, "Steve, this is Lisa. I'm in trouble! You gotta come get me!"

It was not long before my friend Jeff and I were picking up Lisa at the Buttles Avenue crack house. Minutes after we sped away with her, the enraged drug dealer showed up on Buttles and shot someone he mistook for Lisa.

Not having a game plan for this type of situation, I took Lisa to my house. We didn't have a spare bedroom, so Lisa slept on the floor of our living room.

The scene was a little comical when our teenage son woke up Christmas morning only to discover a blonde, teenage hooker asleep under the Christmas tree. For a minute, I was almost "Dad of the Year."

The sobering reality was that there was a killer who wanted this girl, and he knew I had her. We were not quite certain how much danger we faced.

We called on some trusted friends who were willing to "go on a little farther," giving up part of their Christmas Day in order to help us. Moving Lisa from family to family and home to home for several days, we managed to keep her safe from harm.

With some work, we found a long-term home for Lisa—a place where she could move forward in the new life that was God's Christmas gift to her.

The last time she called me, that new Lisa was on the other end, and this time the conversation began, "Steve, this is Lisa. I'm not in trouble. Thank you."

That phone call at 11:30 p.m. on Christmas Eve turned out not to be such a bad inconvenience after all.

Read Luke 1:26–38.

The phone call from Lisa was an inconvenience. God's plan usually calls for a change in our plans: a dinner date broken, a trip to someplace we would rather not go, a reallocation of money we wanted to use for something fun. He doesn't seem to mind inconveniencing us.

The story of the birth of Jesus is a tale of inconvenience.

Mary and Joseph, the innkeeper, the Bethlehem shepherds, and the wise men all found themselves inconvenienced by God's plan.

1. The angel Gabriel's message to Mary was not only inconvenient, it radically changed her life plan. Taking that into consideration, how would you characterize Mary's response in Luke 1:38?
2. God's plan for Lisa's life gave her a new life as a new creation (person). In what ways have you experienced a new life as a result of God's plan for you?
3. Are there ways in which God is calling you to be inconvenienced? If not, why not?

Prayer

Lift me up into your presence, comforting God, for I seek a homeland with you, where your promises find fulfillment and my intentions are faithfully lived out.

Melt me, mold me, fill me, and use me in your perfect design this day.

Help me to listen carefully and act wisely, keeping me alert to discern your purposes in all I do and say so I can realize the best you have for me today and every day.

Enliven me so that when I see or hear your people suffering, I will act. Replace any hesitation to serve with a passion born of authentic faith.

O Spirit of the living God, fall afresh on me this day.

Thanks be to God, Amen.

Scan the QR Code for a bonus video.

> Wherever he went—in villages, cities, or
> the countryside—they brought the sick out
> to the marketplaces. They begged him to let
> the sick touch at least the fringe of his robe,
> and all who touched him were healed.
>
> —MARK 6:56 (NLT)

GOD'S BEAUTY MARK

"Pastor Steve! Do you remember us?"

I hate it when someone asks me that question.

Wanda and I were passing out gifts at our annual Christmas Eve party. Our little storefront on High Street was crowded with almost one hundred people who were homeless, or not too far from being there.

And yet, it was Christmas. Everything was festive. I knew everyone by name—almost everyone, that is.

Everyone except this woman who was certain I would remember her.

The man and young girl behind her were not prompting my memory either.

I knew I should know them, but my mind was drawing a blank. Embarrassing! After an awkward few moments of silence, I confessed. "I'm sorry. I know I should know you, but you are going to have to give me a little help."

"You prayed for us over at Second Avenue school yard," she began. That was all it took! How could I have forgotten?

It had been a big community outreach, maybe five years ago. We had given away a semi-load of ladies brand new, name brand, high fashion clothing. Over four hundred people showed up.

Wanda and I were assigned to lead the prayer line, and there had been lots of people wanting prayer. But, I would never forget this woman. Actually, it was her little girl who would move me to tears every time I thought of her.

The woman, angry and frustrated, had cried, "A pit bull done this to my baby!" Clinging to her leg was a precious five-year-old girl whose face looked like it had been run through a meat grinder. It was all I could stomach to look at the carnage that had recently been this child's face.

"Preacher," she continued, "the doctor said it would take over fifty-thousand-dollars of surgery to fix her face! And we ain't got a dime! On top of that, my old man left us. What are we gonna do?"

As I looked at the terrified little girl, I had to fight back the urge to throw up. The mess that, just a couple of days before, was a child's rosy complexion, now bore more resemblance to raw hamburger.

I have learned that how we first react when faced with a crisis is critical to the outcome of that crisis. I knew that the manner in which I reacted to the crisis of this family's life was more important than the revulsion I was feeling. Choking back our tears, Wanda and I knelt down by the child as I asked, "Honey, may I put my arms around you?"

Making certain to be gentle, I began to pray for God to completely restore her face and to heal all of her hurts and injuries. I prayed that the same power with which Jesus healed people would flow into this little girl and heal her perfectly. I prayed over her like she was my baby. I prayed for the family to have every resource they needed. Almost as an afterthought, I prayed for the woman's husband to return to his family as well.

"Remember what her face looked like?" The woman's voice snapped me back to the reality of our present setting. "Well, look at her now!"

There, standing before me, was a girl with as beautiful and perfect a face as I have ever seen. God had completely healed her face!

"Preacher, her face started healing up an' we never spent another cent on a doctor's visit! Look, God even left her a beauty mark!"

I had to look closely, but just below the left corner of her mouth was one tiny dimple—God's beauty mark indeed—a dimple that would serve as an indelible little reminder of God's presence and power in her life.

"And remember my old man?" Reaching around and grabbing the man behind her she exclaimed, "Look! He come home too!"

That's the last time I recall ever seeing that woman, man, and child. I have no idea what became of that beautiful girl. However, I do know this: she has traveled her journey of life carrying God's beauty mark on her face.

Read Luke 2:12.

Neither the Bethlehem shepherds nor anyone else who witnessed the "baby lying in a manger" could have foretold the scars Jesus would bear from the wounds he would suffer fulfilling his mission, "going on a little farther" for us as the Savior of humankind (See Mark 15:16–23).

1. As you think about the wounds Jesus suffered, in what ways can you see his scars serving as beauty marks from God?
2. If we think about it, we all experience little beauty marks from God—seemingly insignificant little reminders signifying God's presence in our lives. What can you identify as God's beauty marks in your own life?

Prayer

Awesome God, in the light of this new day, reveal to me ways that I can profess my faith openly as a witness with a strong conviction to say what I believe.

Open my eyes to the surprises you have in store for me today. Make me aware that they are not the work of human hands but rather of your love in action.

So often I have trouble not only believing what I see but believing what I affirm.

O God, I affirm your power, yet I often act surprised when it is revealed throughout the world. I affirm the power of prayer but secretly wonder what really healed the person for whom I prayed. Why am I so surprised when what I affirm really happens?

Send your loving Spirit upon me and surprise me with your healing power as I continue to grow, move forward, and pray with Jesus.

Thanks be to God, Amen.

Scan the QR Code for a bonus video.

> "I tell you the truth," Jesus said, "this poor widow has given more than all the rest of them. For they have given a tiny part of their surplus, but she, poor as she is, has given everything she has."
>
> —LUKE 21:3–4 (NLT)

DOC'S HOLIDAY

There is an adage that says, "Dynamite comes in small packages." That's a fitting description of Doc Holiday.

A study in contradictions, Doc was small but mighty, short-fused, and heavy-tempered. He knew and understood life on the inside and life on the streets. He once stuck a pistol into a man's chest and shot him straight through the heart. That landed him in prison for quite a while. Twice, I removed brass knuckles from his possession. That landed him on my growing list of street characters who I hoped to keep on my good side.

I've known some tough street characters through the years, many with names that spoke to their personas: an Irishman named Cochise, an African American named Geronimo, Bobby Little, who wasn't little, and Bobby Stout, who wasn't stout. Then there was Bulldog, Angel, Big Momma, White Mike, Thief, and so on. But none was any tougher, or any more dangerous, than Doc Holiday.

Unlike many people on the streets who are dangerous as a way to mask their cowardice, Doc was dangerous because he was dangerous. He was a rough-and-tumble street fighter who wasn't afraid of anyone or anything. He made his home under the East Broad Street Bridge where he served as the "mayor" of a small band of thugs called the River Rats.

Like many people of the streets, Doc had his own sense of right and wrong and his own brand of justice.

One night, while I was teaching a Bible study, a man sitting in the back row pulled out a bottle and took a swig of it.

Seeing this, Doc leapt to his feet, took two steps toward the man and unleashed a punch that broke the man's nose, blacked both his eyes, and sent him into the brick wall behind him. Glaring at the stunned man, Doc growled, "This here is God's joint! Now you show some respect!"

For some reason, Doc liked me and, despite my message of peace and his tendency toward violence, he listened to me. More than once he told me, "Steve, you preach good. It makes sense. You keep talking to me."

I knew better than to think Doc's words were a compliment. Doc didn't give compliments. Instead, Doc gave me a direct order, one that I didn't take lightly (and not just because of the brass knuckles). Whenever I had the chance, I shared God's message with Doc.

At some point, Doc accepted Jesus as his Lord and Savior, and over the months and through the years, Doc—though still tough with an iron fist—began to change.

One of the ways God was working in Doc came to light at our annual Christmas party. Held just before Christmas, it was as close to a gala as any of our friends would ever get. It was a ticketed event, and guests had to show their tickets to gain admission. After a sumptuous feast, they exchanged their tickets for gift bags filled with new sleeping bags, tents, hoodies, gloves, socks, and other items necessary for outdoor survival.

We gave people their tickets several days before the party and warned them not to lose them—and treasure that ticket they did. For most of our guests, it was the only Christmas they would receive.

This particular night, Doc was standing in line waiting to redeem his ticket. He was looking forward to getting a new supply of items that might make the difference between his surviving or perishing during the winter months.

While waiting, a man named Willie Dog burst into the room. Willie Dog was a Vietnam vet who, mentally speaking, never came home from the war.

While Doc lived under the East Broad Street Bridge, Willie Dog lived under the West Broad Street Bridge. Though their bridges were separated by several miles, Doc and Willie were friends.

Approaching Doc, Willie moaned, "Doc, I lost my ticket!! Man, what am I going to do? Without that stuff they give me at Christmas, man, I ain't gonna make it!"

Fully understanding Willie's desperate reality, Doc held up his ticket and handed it to Willie. "Here Dog, take mine. Merry Christmas!"

With that, Doc turned around and walked out into the cold December night.

The journey of Doc's life had been rough and often brutal. But Doc had come to a new place on his journey of life—a place where the needs of a friend were more important to him than his own needs. It was a place where he was willing to "go on a little farther" by setting aside his own needs for the sake of someone else. It takes a truly tough man to do that—not tough in the physical sense, but tough in the heart. It takes a man who can be tender-hearted toward others and tough enough to live it out. That was Doc: tough on the inside and out.

About thirty days after that Christmas, we received a letter at our little center. The letter was addressed to the man we knew as Doc Holiday. Within the letter, an attorney from North Carolina informed Doc that a relative had died and left him his estate, a property that included a small farm with a nice home on it.

That Christmas, Doc Holiday rescued Willie from the deadly worst of winter's brutality. He stepped up in Willie's greatest time of need. A month later, God met Doc's greatest need. Through the gift of the property in North Carolina, God forever delivered Doc from having to live on the streets.

Finally living up to his name, Doc experienced quite a holiday.

Read Matthew 2:1–12.

The wise men from the East brought precious gifts to Jesus. Doc Holiday gave a most generous gift to Willie Dog on Christmas Eve.

1. In our verse at the top of the page, a widow gave a couple of pennies. In what way was each of these costly, valuable, and precious?
2. Are there parallels that can be drawn between Doc's action and that of the poor widow in our theme verse (Luke 21:3–4)?

Prayer

Thank you, Creator God, for bringing light and warmth to a dreary and hurting world. I come asking for another chance. You said to ask. I was afraid to speak. You said seek. I had my doubts. You said knock. Why did I stop before I reached the door?

It is only when I have claimed my own place in your love that I can experience this all-embracing, non-comparing love and feel safe, not only with you but also with my brothers and sisters. I must take to heart that you call me your beloved. The voice that calls me will give me words to bless others and reveal to them that they too are loved by you.

I ask for another chance to seek forgiveness and your will and boldly knock upon your door. Loving God, there is no greater love than the love expressed when one gives up one's life for the sake of another.

Thanks be to God, Amen.

Scan the QR Code for a bonus video.

Our first ministry center, located at 1129 N. High Street.

"The Wall Street Dumpster"—Hardly the Stock Market. Rather, a dark alley hiding place for a teenage hooker, and the dying place for more than one person.

This landmark sign is a beacon of hope to the hurting. The Dream Center motto is, "Find a need and meet it. Find a hurt and heal it."

Plaque outside Columbus Dream Center. A promise from God repeated so often that it has become a byline.

Searching for anything that can help
him survive another day.

Ministry begins before the doors of
the Dream Center open.

Life on the streets is exhausting. He is sleeping outside
the Dream Center because he feels safe there.

Time has changed our appearance, but time
has not changed the heart of what we do.

> Today I have given you the choice between life
> and death, between blessings and curses. Now
> I call on heaven and earth to witness the choice
> you make. Oh, that you would choose life, so
> that you and your descendants might live.
>
> —DEUTERONOMY 30:19 (NLT)

THE GIRL AT THE DUMPSTER

*Decision points: events and moments that direct, alter, and shape
our lives. Decision points can come from experiences as dramatic as
"9/11" or as simple as a chat with grandpa. Decision points often
result in our moving toward something—a career, a goal, or a
significant relationship. Decision points can result in our walking
away from something, perhaps something we fear: an addiction, a
relationship, or even a personal failure.*

*As life-altering and important as decision points can be, they often
come when we are least expecting them, at the most unlikely places.
They can even occur at a garbage dumpster located in an inner-city
alley at 3:00 a.m. on Christmas morning.*

It was early Christmas morning, 2:30 a.m. to be exact. I
awakened and slipped out of our home, unnoticed. At last, I
was alone.

Christmas is supposed to be a time of great joy and celebration. But for me, it was a season of turmoil. The nature of our work had brought a series of threats against my life and a string of acts of vandalism against our property. There had been bomb threats, fires set, windows broken, and pit bulls turned loose in our Children's Ministry Area. There was at least one contract on my life. The police cautioned me that I should not go anywhere alone.

After weeks of feeling restricted, as though I couldn't even cross the street without supervision, I was fed up. I didn't care about the Christmas spirit; I just wanted to be out somewhere, on my own.

The bed of my truck was filled with trash and junk I wanted to throw away. With little regard for the risk I was taking by going out alone into an area of the city where there were people who wanted to kill me, I headed toward our ministry center in what was then the notorious Short North District of Columbus. There, behind our storefront, located in a dark and seemingly empty alley known as Wall Street, sat our dumpster.

The dumpster was located in a small alcove. There was enough space behind the dumpster for homeless people to shelter themselves, and many did.

I once identified the body of a murder victim found there by the police: a partially-clothed homeless man with evident head wounds. Wall Street was a dangerous place. Being there alone at night had cost more than one person his life.

As I got out of the truck and started to unload the junk into that dumpster, the scene bore no resemblance to the poem "The Night Before Christmas"—until, "When what to my wondering eyes should appear?" was not "A miniature sleigh and eight tiny reindeer," *but a girl walking out from behind the dumpster.*

No older than sixteen, she was not one of Santa's elves. Her clothing told the story that she was definitely "on the streets." Even in the early morning darkness, I could tell this girl was exceptionally pretty. Yet the bruises on her face, her discolored lip, and a black eye told a Christmas story that did not come from the pages of the Bible, or the pen of Clement Clarke Moore.

The police have told me that when a child or teenager lands on the streets of Columbus, Ohio, he or she will be "recruited" by sex traffickers within four hours. This child was some trafficker's slave. Her wounds were a tale of an abusive handler or a "trick gone bad."

Attempting to appear as sophisticated and sexy as one can appear while crawling out from behind a dumpster, she inquired, "Mister, would you like me to show you a real good time?"

Stunned by the moment, I thought, *Oh God, this is somebody's daughter! A child who should be home with loving parents, "all snuggled in her bed," dreaming of Christmas morning and waiting to get up and open presents! Instead, she's down here behind a dumpster. She is sleeping in a place where homeless men go to relieve themselves. She's at risk of freezing while waiting for someone, anyone, who will pay her a few dollars for a real good time.*

Trying to grasp how far this was from "The Night Before Christmas" or "Silent Night, Holy Night, all is calm, all is bright" I attempted to gather my composure.

"Sweetheart, sit down on the tailgate of my truck and let's visit for just a minute."

I grabbed an emergency blanket that I kept in my truck with which she could warm herself. Eyeing me, the truck bed, and the blanket, she sensed an all-too-familiar danger.

Looking at me with fear and mistrust she asked, "What do you want me to do mister?"

What did I want her to do?

My mind ran to, *If a police car comes down the alley right now, it won't matter what either one of us is doing. I'm going to jail, and the headlines won't be pretty!*

I was also keenly aware of the possibility that a pimp could be lurking in the shadows, waiting to mug me.

This girl had not been on the street too long. While she bore some of the marks of the life she was leading, the streets had not yet made her hard or calloused.

Tears welled in the eyes of both of us as we talked. Her pain went far beyond deep.

As one who many years before had spent a Christmas locked away in a drug rehab center, I shared with her from the innermost depths of my heart:

Regardless of where you are at the moment, it's okay. The reason it's okay is because God is waiting to accept you and help you right where you are.

Living in the penthouse or the tent house, it doesn't matter.

Tucked in a nice, warm bed at home or sleeping behind a dumpster in one of the most dangerous alleys in town, either way, God wants to wrap his loving arms around you—and you don't have to do anything except allow him to do that.

The other great truth I shared with the teenage girl is as important as the first.

God loves you far too much to leave you where you are. If you allow God to lead, he will take you places you could never go on your own.

God has a plan for your life. In his own words, he said it is a "plan for your good, to give you a peace and a hope" (Jeremiah 29:11). God wants to give you a peace and a hope.

The teenage girl and I talked for fifteen minutes. One quarter of one hour, on an early Christmas morning.

She walked out from behind a dumpster. Her plan was to have sex with a stranger and get paid a few dollars. That's not a very good plan for life's journey.

She walked out from behind a dumpster and squarely into a decision point. Instead of cheap sex with someone she didn't know, she encountered God's love and a chance to set her life on an entirely different path. That is a serious decision point.

She allowed me to pray for her. Then, without voicing any decision, she walked off into the wintery night.

I never saw her again.

The girl at the dumpster was very real. Throughout the years, I have thought of her many times. Even today she haunts my memory.

Did she decide to allow God to enter her life, or did she put it off? What became of her? Did she wind up leading a wholesome, happy, fulfilling life? Or did she become just another kid found dead in a back street alley?

That's the thing about decision points. No matter what we decide, we have to live with the outcome.

Read Joshua 24:15.

The most important decision point a person can face is the decision to make Jesus his or her Lord, the leader of his or her life. If we get that decision right, God can guide us in making all the others.

Making Jesus our Lord is a simple prayer: *Dear God, Please come into my life. I accept your forgiveness of all my sins. I ask Jesus to be the Lord of my life. Please guide me in all I do. I pray in Jesus's name, Amen.*

1. How did you come to that decision point in your life? If you have not come to that already, what's stopping you? You can pray that prayer right now.
2. Are you currently facing decision points in which you find it difficult to trust God?

Prayer

Grant me this day, O God. Clear my sight each day so that I can see the way I ought to take my journey. When the decision point confronts me, give me the courage and perseverance to follow it to the end.

Help me to live in such a way that my conduct makes it plain that I belong to you.

Give me the humility to ask what is your will for me, and give me the trust and obedience to say, "Your will be done."

Through Jesus Christ our Lord, Amen

Scan the QR Code for a bonus video.

> **Are not all angels ministering spirits sent to serve those who will inherit salvation?**
>
> —HEBREWS 1:14 (NIV)

THE MAN ON THE STATEHOUSE STEPS

It was Christmas Eve, a night to celebrate God coming to earth in the form of a baby. It was a time for festivity, food, and giving gifts. But the sub-freezing temperature, icy winds, and blowing snow were not adding to the Christmas spirit. Instead, they only added to the loneliness, anxiety, and depression often felt by those who live on the land.

It had been a hard night at our little center on High Street. Our crowd had been small for Christmas Eve. Neither the music nor the preaching was very good. I should know. I did both of them.

The dinner wasn't all that gourmet. People didn't seem to be all that appreciative of the gifts we gave them. To make matters worse, both of my parents were hospitalized in separate cities almost a thousand miles from where I was.

I thought, *Why did I even have to be here?* My Christmas attitude was definitely "Bah, humbug!"

Midnight was fast approaching, the evening activities were concluded, and all of our volunteers and staff were eager to get to one place and one place only—home.

Then almost suddenly, there they were!

An old jalopy of a car rumbled to a stop across High Street, and a young couple exited and started across the street, heading right for our door. They didn't even have coats! What was that in their arms? A baby? Out in weather like this?

A young couple with a baby out in the cold on Christmas Eve? Were we replaying a storyline torn from the pages of the New Testament itself? I felt a little like the storied innkeeper of Bethlehem (of whom the Bible bears no record) when I opened our door to let them in.

Why were they here?

I soon learned that their story was truly a Christmas miracle.

Their baby had been at Nationwide Children's Hospital for several weeks. They had been going back and forth between their home in a little village an hour north of Columbus and the hospital. At 8:00 p.m. on Christmas Eve the doctors came in and told them they were dismissing their baby to go home. I didn't know doctors even worked Christmas Eve!

The problem was that they weren't expecting to go home.

They had planned to spend the night in the hospital.

They didn't have money for a room or for food.

They didn't have any money—period.

The heater in their car was broken, and the gas gauge was pushing empty. They were completely stuck on a cold Christmas Eve and didn't know what to do.

Not really knowing why they were doing it, they drove a short distance from the hospital down to the Ohio State Capitol Building. By this time, it was 11:00 p.m. when they parked the car on the empty street and began to walk around the completely deserted Statehouse.

As they came around the west side of the building, a man wearing a coat and sweatshirt bearing our ministry logo stood on the Statehouse steps. He was sweeping the snow off the steps.

He stopped sweeping, leaned on his broom, and inquired of them as to how he might help. They told him their predicament, adding that they didn't know why they were at the Statehouse.

With a reassuring smile he told them, "Go to 1203 North High Street. There are people there who are waiting to serve you."

Still not understanding why, they did just as he instructed.

And just when we were hopeful that the night was over, that's when God gave us the opportunity to "go on a little farther."

We quickly got them warmed with blankets and hot chocolate. We outfitted them with coats and hoodies. We were out of gloves so we fashioned socks to serve as mittens.

We loaded their car with groceries and Christmas presents galore. A stop at the all-night gas station across the street filled the tank on the old car. We all reached in our pockets and gave them the money that we had.

We shared with them the Good News of salvation through Jesus and that God wants to accept and embrace us right where we are, just as we are. It's not that we deserve God's love; he gives it to us freely.

Even though they were stuck that night, with seemingly no way out, God loved them too much to leave them there. He used a man sweeping the snow off the steps of the completely vacant Ohio Statehouse to intervene in their situation.

You see, if we will allow God to lead us, he will take us places we could never go on our own.

As we wished them well and sent them off with a hearty "Merry Christmas," there was one thing we didn't tell them.

Only our staff and volunteers have branded items like the ones that the man sweeping the steps was wearing. But we didn't have anyone out on the street or working at the Statehouse that night. Based on their description, not one of us recognized who the man might be.

Besides, who sweeps the snow off the Statehouse steps at 11:00 p.m. on Christmas Eve?

Read Luke 1:11–20.

The New Testament accounts of Matthew and Luke regarding the birth of Jesus contain six occasions in which angels are sent as heavenly messengers.

The Bible tells us that angels are "ministering spirits sent to serve those who will inherit salvation" (Hebrews 1:14, NLT).

1. Have you experienced an instance when you were the recipient of assistance or help that you consider to have been divine in nature because it could not be explained in human logic?
2. Have you ever experienced a time when you feel you might have encountered an angel?

Prayer

You are truly the God of surprises, and I greet this new day with anticipation.

Awaken me to your presence, O God, that I might be ready for the unexpected.

God of promise, how often will I meet you today in the faces I see? How often will I entertain angels unaware?

Let me be mindful, O God, that when I encounter others, I encounter you!

Your love, O God, enfolds me.

In Jesus's name I pray, Amen.

Scan the QR Code for a bonus video.

One of [the ten lepers], when he saw that he
was healed, came back to Jesus, shouting,
"Praise God!" He fell on the ground at Jesus'
feet, thanking him for what he had done.

—LUKE 17:15–16 (NLT)

BLANKETS OF THANKS

"Here! Let me help you with that!" It was a blustery, wintery day, the kind we often get in Ohio a week before Christmas.

An older woman was trying with all her might to drag, carry, or pull two large trash bags through the front door of my corner bookstore on West Fifth Avenue in Columbus.

I was not surprised to learn that the bags contained blankets—new blankets destined for our ministry in the Short North District of the city.

It was part of a project called Blanket Columbus. With the help of local media, we were gathering one thousand new blankets that would be distributed to people living on the land and to families that could not afford blankets.

My bookstore, The Amen Corner, was a designated drop-off point for the blankets.

When we finished wrestling the two bags of blankets into the building, I offered the woman a cup of coffee to ease the winter chill. I learned there were twenty new blankets in the bags and that the woman had never before been to my store.

She had no idea I operated the ministry that would be receiving the blankets. To her, I was just the guy behind the counter in the bookstore.

Curious as to the unusually large number of blankets she was delivering, I inquired, "So, tell me about these blankets?"

I was anything but prepared for the story she told me.

"You know, it's really interesting," she said. "We live about an hour north of here. Yesterday, I was over at my daughter's house. We were in her kitchen where she was listening to the radio while she was making some homemade vegetable soup. An announcement came on the radio about the ministry needing these blankets down here in Columbus.

"Well, my daughter stopped in her tracks. She put down what she was doing, and said, 'Mom, those are the folks who rescued us four years ago on Christmas Eve when Becca was released from the hospital.' (See the story "The Man on the Statehouse Steps.")

"'Mom, those people saved our lives! We gotta help them!'"

Still not knowing that I led the ministry to whom the blankets were being given, or my role in the Christmas Eve in question, the woman pointed to the blankets and said, "So here they are. I wish I could thank those folks for rescuing my family!"

I nodded my head and said, "Yes ma'am, I will let them know. And by the way, you did just say *thank you.*"

The Blanket Columbus initiative involved our receiving over one thousand new blankets. Those blankets were distributed to people living in homeless camps and the worst of inner-city housing. Every one of the blankets was a precious gift given to us that enabled us to help others.

Yet the twenty brought to the bookstore by that woman were, to me, the most precious of all. They were a Thanksgiving offering from someone God had rescued, given in order that God might rescue others.

Read Luke 2:25–38.

Simeon and Anna were people of whom we know little, yet they were among the first to recognize Jesus for who he was. In recognizing Jesus as the Savior of humankind, they gave thanks to God.

In seeing the infant Jesus, Simeon realized the fulfillment of a promise God had given him.

1. What was that promise, and how did Simeon respond?
2. Through the gift of twenty blankets, a family expressed their thankfulness for God rescuing them in a time of trouble. Are there people to whom you should express your thankfulness for God intervening on your behalf?

Prayer

Generous God, sometimes life gets me down and I find it difficult to see things for which to be thankful.

Open my eyes to see the gifts you have placed in my life.

I'm going to start by thanking you for loving me enough that you came to earth and died so that I might have eternal life.

May I, without fear or embarrassment, model a lifestyle based on Christ's love.

It is through you and with you that I can design my day for real living, with eyes for seeing your wonders, ears for hearing your call to faith, and a heart that believes.

O God of surprising grace, give me some sign as to where you will be waiting for me today.

It is in faith I move in your direction to find your presence and surprises.

Thanks be to God, Amen.

Scan the QR Code for a bonus video.

> *"For I know the plans I have for you,"* says
> the Lord. *"They are plans for good and not for
> disaster, to give you a future and a hope."*
> —JEREMIAH 29:11 (NLT)

CHRISTMAS LEMONADE

It was going to be just another freezing Friday night in December, a night I would spend riding in an old school bus across Ohio's winter landscape.

With decades of coaching high school basketball behind me, the bus ride promised two, and only two, guarantees:

1. The bus would smell of sweaty boys; and
2. It would be cold.

I was stepping on the bus when the phone call came. Our athletic director said the game was canceled.

"Coach, they say it's snowing like crazy there! They're expecting twelve to fourteen inches."

"It looks like we're going to get it too! Coach, if I were you, I'd pack it in and enjoy a quiet Christmas season night at home."

As good as a night off sounded, my mind turned to our homeless center located in the Short North District of Columbus, Ohio.

Wanda and I were supposed to have the night off. I was going to coach and she was going to wrap gifts at home.

The weather advisory was urging people not to travel. The forecasters were saying to just go home and stay there.

Everything in me wanted to do just that.

Still, I knew what a storm like this could do to the homeless population in our city.

I called Wanda. "Hey, there is a big snow storm headed our way. I know we are not supposed to have to work tonight, but the homeless don't get the night off. So we had best head to the Short North and get prepared."

"Sure thing honey." I was always amazed that she would call me "honey," even when I asked her to drop her plans and head out into the cold. She was always so willing to "go on a little farther" in order to help our friends who were living on the land.

"Steve," she continued, "you know what this means? The group bringing the meal for tonight will probably cancel, and some of our staff won't feel safe driving into the city tonight. It's going to be a pretty tough night."

"You're right. Pack a bag to stay warm, and be ready to spend the night. I don't know what we'll do to feed people, but we'll just figure it out as we go. It's just a bunch of lemons. So, let's make some Christmas lemonade."

Wanda and I both prayed as we made the drive down into the notorious Short North District. Our motto had long been, "Pray as you go, and go as you pray." The ministry demands didn't afford us the time to stop and pray.

By the time we reached our little center on High Street, the snow was beginning to pile up—four inches...five inches...six inches, and still no sign of stopping.

Sure enough, the group scheduled to bring the food for the night called and canceled.

All of our staff for that night called in and asked for the night off.

Indeed it was going to be a very challenging night.

I prayed, "God, You're going to have to make some really good lemonade, 'cause this is one ugly bunch of lemons!"

Then, in walked Jeff and Martha, long-time volunteer staff workers. They were not on the schedule for tonight, but Jeff said, "We just didn't want to miss an opportunity like this one."

Well, we had an opportunity!

Thirty-two homeless people hiked into our center that night. Some came from camps as far as five miles away. Some had never been to our center before that night. When I asked why they came to our place, they said, "We heard that no matter how bad it gets, you guys are always here for people living on the land."

Martha and Wanda made certain that people received hot coffee and snacks, while Jeff put together a short Bible message for the evening. I got on the phone and found a pizza shop that was still open. The proprietor was snowed in and only too glad to get an order for twenty large pies.

By that time, the snow was too deep for driving, so I deputized two homeless guys, Curtis and Sellers, to hike the half-mile to the shop with me and bring back the pizzas.

What a glorious batch of Christmas lemonade it turned out to be!

While Curtis, Sellers, and I were hiking to get the pizzas, Jeff, Martha, and Wanda led eighteen people to Christ! All of the first-time-attendees came to faith that night!

Even though the twenty large pizzas disappeared in no time, the fun and the fellowship went well into the night.

Eventually our guests departed—hiking back into their camps under bridges or down by the railroad tracks, or sleeping in dumpsters or abandoned shacks. Jeff, Martha, Wanda, and I watched with tearful eyes as our friends disappeared into the snowy darkness.

It was truly a night to remember. Jeff, Martha, Wanda, and I recognized that God had just taken each of us "a little farther" out of our comfort zones. We all agreed that our favorite treat for that Christmas season was the night God made "Christmas lemonade."

Read Luke 2:4–7.

Just like Joseph, Mary, Zechariah, and the Bethlehem shepherds, when God throws us a change in plans, we tend to react with fear.

1. For Joseph and Mary, the trip to Bethlehem probably looked like a lemon. It was a long walk, and there is no biblical evidence that Mary rode a donkey. She was pregnant, there was no place for them to stay, and she birthed her baby in a barn. In what ways do you see that day turning a bunch of lemons into lemonade?
2. Can you recall a time in your life when God turned a bunch of lemons into lemonade?

Prayer

O gentle God, you want me to live a life of order, not chaos. There is to be a time and season for everything—a rhythm.

> Just as night follows day and spring follows winter, there is a time for giving birth and a time for dying, a time for planting and a time for uprooting what was planted, a time for tearing down and a time for building up, a time for crying and a time for laughing, a time for mourning and a time for dancing. (Ecclesiastes 3:2–4 CEB)

O God, I know that I can only accomplish order and rhythm on the outside if there is order and rhythm in my heart. I pray with the hymn writer, John Greenleaf Whittier: "Drop thy still dews of quietness, 'til all our striving cease; take from our souls the strain and stress, and let our ordered lives confess the beauty of thy peace."

Jesus wants us to know that we are not loved because we have values; rather, we have values because we are loved.

Thanks be to God, Amen.

Scan the QR Code for a bonus video.

> **For he will order his angels to**
> **protect you wherever you go.**
>
> —PSALM 91:11 (NLT)

MERRY CHRISTMAS, RAYSHAWN

It was four days until Christmas. In the dead of night, I was standing at one of the most dangerous intersections in Columbus, where only the night before a brutal murder had occurred.

To make matters worse, that very afternoon, I had been diagnosed with a life-threatening heart condition. In fact, I would die the next day while on the surgeon's table. Obviously, my death was not permanent.

The doctor ordered me to stay home and rest. So why was I out there risking my life in the freezing cold?

Earlier in the evening my phone rang and I answered. It was Donelle. She was the working, single mother of two boys, CJ and Rayshawn, both of whom attended our teen program.

Even though Rayshawn was about fifteen years old, he looked every inch a man. Like many adolescents, Rayshawn was searching for a place to belong. Despite Donelle doing all she could to keep track of two teenage boys, Rayshawn began gravitating toward guys who were connected to one of the major gangs in our city. The gang was blood-in, blood-out, meaning you take someone else's blood to get in and you give your own blood to get out.

Donelle was frantic. Rayshawn had run away and was going through the early stages of gang initiation in an east-end drug house. She begged me to go get him out before it was too late. I didn't tell her, but I knew it was already too late. Still, I heard in my heart, *He went on a little farther.* So I told Donelle I would go.

I instructed Donelle to park her van around the corner, just within eyesight of the drug house. I told her that just as soon as she saw Rayshawn outside she was to quickly drive up in front of the house. I warned her that once Rayshawn got in the car, they needed to get out of there immediately. I told her, "Don't wait for me! My guardian angel Spike will look out for me!"

So there I was, standing by myself in front of a gang's drug house, all alone except for Spike, my guardian angel.

The sub-freezing night air made my chest hurt so badly that I struggled to walk up to the house. A young man approached. He had been posted as a sentry to keep everyone away from the gang's house. Before either one of us could grasp what was going on, he began confessing to me a murder he committed. Within a few minutes, I laid my hands on him and prayed as he asked Jesus to come into his life and forgive all that he had done.

Sensing the moment was right, I went up on the porch, knocked on the door of the drug house and announced, "I've come to get Rayshawn. Let me have him!"

Inside, I heard the chambering of automatic weapons. Then a voice called out, "Hey dude! You the 5-0?"

"No," I replied. "I'm Rayshawn's pastor. I've come to take him home."

There was a definite pause. Then, "Dude! Don't you know we will kill you?"

To that I replied, "We can do this the hard way or the easy way. You can kill me. Understand, I really don't care. But if you kill me, that is going to draw a lot of attention to this place. Or you can just give Rayshawn to me, and you don't ever have to hear from me again. Either way, Rayshawn is leaving. Now, you choose!"

I heard the door unlock. Then as it slowly opened, I saw a very frightened Rayshawn cowering just inside the door.

Suddenly, it was as though an angel (Spike?) reached through the door, grabbed Rayshawn, and jerked him out of that house!

As I turned to the street, his mom drove up. I threw him into the car, and she sped away.

With that, I said, "Merry Christmas, Rayshawn! Let's go home, Spike."

Read Luke 2:13–14.

1. Angels sent by God appear six times during the Bible accounts of the events leading to and closely following the birth of Jesus. Can you name the angels? (Hint: Luke 1:11–20, Luke 1:26–38, Matthew 1:20–24, Luke 2:8–20, Matthew 2:13–14, Matthew 2:19–20)
2. Have you had a time when you were in danger and felt like God watched over you in a supernatural manner or possibly sent an angel to intervene?

Prayer

O God of grace, there are times I do not know what to say to myself or to you. What is the truth of my life? I am too scared to see and too proud to share. Prod me gently, yet insistently, to look at myself with honesty.

I realize I am a complex creature and my life is confused and overrun, my spirit is clouded and crippled. Help me to clear the garbage away so that I might see clearly and hear plainly. Loosen the chains that hold me down so that I might straighten up. Unwind what binds me so that I might find movement toward you once again, and feel free to move toward myself and others, sharing the gift of your love.

Thanks be to God, Amen.

Scan the QR Code for a bonus video.

> **"So now I am giving you a new commandment:
> Love each other. Just as I have loved
> you, you should love each other."**
>
> —JOHN 13:34 (NLT)

WE WOULDN'T HAD NO CHRISTMAS

It was our first "Short North Christmas Eve." A hard sleet pelted the ground, and in our little High Street center, the "stockings were hung by the chimney with care," in hopes that a crowd would be gathering there.

Parked outside was the closest thing we had to Santa's sleigh: two box vans filled with gifts, groceries, and hygiene kits. There would be hoodies, gloves, socks, and other life necessities for all. Tents, tarps, and sleeping bags awaited those who lived on the land.

The question in my mind was, *Would anyone venture out in this weather for a Christmas Eve party?*

Much to my surprise and delight, venture out they did!

I had never seen such a stream of soaked, shivering people. Soon a crowd of one hundred twenty-five filled a space prepared to hold only sixty. We seated the ones we could, but most had to stand.

It was a Christmas Eve for the ages, filled with carols and food, gifts and food, and festivities and food. Did I mention the food?

As the party was winding down, a woman with three little ones in tow approached me. A baby and a toddler were in well-used strollers and a five-year-old was helping her push them.

"Mister," she said, "I got no way to get my gifts home. It's icy 'n slick. Them bags are too big for me to carry. I got all I can handle with these kids."

Glancing at the two full strollers, her words rang true: she had all she could handle.

"Give me your address and your gifts. I will drop them off to you when I leave."

With that, I put her gifts in the back of one of the box vans. Problem solved—or so I thought.

Driving home from the party proved to be a real challenge. For one thing, it was late—1:30 in the morning, to be exact. Also, the roads were icy and proving treacherous for the big, mostly empty truck.

Not to mention, I was exhausted. More than glad to have the Short North District thirty minutes in my rear-view mirror,

I began thinking about home when an alarm went off in my mind. *I still had that woman's gifts in the back of my truck!*

Looking for an easy way out, I thought, *I'll just deliver the gifts first thing in the morning. After all, it's so late and they'll be asleep by now.*

Then, that still, small voice within me said, "You said you would do it tonight."

Sometimes, I hate that little voice.

Clearly tired, I began talking to myself. "I know. This is not in my plans…I don't have time for this…but it's so inconvenient!" I knew I wasn't going to win this argument.

With a whine, I sighed, "Merry Christmas, hmmft!"

Feeling more like the dwarf Grumpy than Santa's helper, I turned the truck around and began to work my way back into the inner city. The drive seemed to take forever. The streets were narrow and some didn't have road signs. Everything was slick. It was 2:15 Christmas morning when I finally found the right street.

"These houses don't even have numbers on them," I complained. "How am I going to know which place is theirs?"

Then, there it was! A tumbled-down shack by an old railroad track with two small children huddled in the snow out front. The kids were waiting for me. They were counting on me!

As I pulled to a stop in front of their house they exclaimed, "Mister, mister! We thought you wasn't coming!"

"Oh, I wouldn't do that to you." I had just lied.

Carefully, I stepped across the front porch, avoiding the boards that were completely rotted. Entering the front door, the sight before me will forever be etched in my mind.

In the living room was an old sofa with a spring sticking out of it. A naked baby slept on one end. The kitchen had a broken-down table with two, rickety chairs. Everything had seen better days.

A single light bulb illuminated the entire space. I soon learned that they took the light bulb with them as they went from room to room. It was a one light bulb house.

A man rose from one of the kitchen chairs, came across the room and grabbed me by the shoulder. With tears streaming down his face, he sobbed, "Mister, if it wasn't for you, we wouldn't had no Christmas!"

That night God blessed that family with Christmas gifts, but I was the recipient of the best gift. By God's grace, I was given the privilege of helping to make someone else's life better. God's gift to me was to give me the opportunity to learn to "go on a little farther," in order to demonstrate his love by meeting their need.

The way I was given that gift didn't fit into my plans. It wasn't convenient. I had complained and whined about being inconvenienced. My selfish attitude almost caused me to miss the greatest Christmas gift I have ever received.

Often the greatest opportunities we receive and the best life experiences don't fit our plans. They're not comfortable or convenient. That's the price of obeying Jesus's command to "love each other."

Learning to love, truly love, involves learning to put others' needs before our own.

Read Matthew 20:26–28.

1. According to the Bible, how did Jesus demonstrate putting the needs of others before his own needs? (Hint: 2 Corinthians 8:9, Luke 19:10)
2. Can you recall times when, through inconveniencing you, God used you to help make someone else's life better?

Prayer

O Creator of life, I humbly admit that far too often, I fall short of my intentions for myself and your expectations for me.

Through your Spirit, I would touch the needs of the world with goodness, but I often withdraw in fear, anxiety, and self-concern. I would live with integrity and stand for truth, but I am torn with uncertainty. I would warm the lives of others with my love, but I hesitate, wondering if they will love me in return. I would go about my daily task with confidence and thanksgiving, but find myself struggling with self-doubt.

I need your presence if I am to be what I could be and want to be.

O God, remind me each new day that I am forgiven and loved by you.

Thanks be to God, Amen.

Scan the QR Code for a bonus video.

Printed in the United States
by Baker & Taylor Publisher Services